EX CATHEDRA

XXVII

PETER JOANNIDES

Printed in the United States of America

Corrected second printing, 2019

ISBN 978-0-9892536-3-5

www.PetroulisI@gmail.com

AUTHOR'S NOTE

This is the latest in the series of **Ex Cathedras** begun in 1972.

Pursuant to the acknowledgements chronicled in the "Author's Note" of **Ex Cathedra XXVI**, I would like, while I still have time and am able, to add this thank-you.

The following individuals were kind enough to help me financially and see me through the typing, typesetting, and general manuscript preparation phases of **Amán Amán!**: Sotirios Karageorge, Dr. David Scales, Paula Bourdet Radius, Col. Roger Arias, Chris Christopher, Art Driscoll, Sr., members of the Kolantis Family, and Jack Demetree.

Peter Joannides

ALSO BY PETER JOANNIDES

February 10, 2018

Ex Cathedra

27th
Encyclical

von Herrn Doktor Professor Peter Joannides

1

Benjamin Netanyahu: what a sly, squirmy, sophistical, inwardly rabid, unsympathetic character.

2

I cannot think of anyone who is less of a philosopher than Donald J. Trump.

3

I always liked and respected the once President
of Israel, Shimon Peres.

(Besides, he invariably reminded me of my
Uncle John.)

4

Ain't no way, you can get away,

Without the laws of physics to obey.

5

I have to admit, I did enjoy being top handball dog in Jacksonville all those years.

I think Donald Trump should resign.

7

Dreams can be very powerful and profound,

And impossible to understand or explain.

Donald Trump

I can't believe that so many people, ordinary run-of-the-mill people, are beginning to think of this joker as our authentic President.

9

I wonder whatever became of my private pilot's license.

I suddenly lost whatever respect I had for Jon Huntsman.

11

Glibness is a double turn-off when it's in the service of the wrong cause.

How many times did I go to the top of the Empire State Building to have **THE GREAT RENEWAL**.

13

So many parents are grotesqueries,

But their little children don't know this,

And most never will.

14

I've never had much interest in politics (except perhaps in a theoretical, philosophical way).

But I can't help it this time around.

15

I resent Trump, and I resent the boobs who put him there.

16

Would you believe it, here I am presumably an educated man, some would even say a well-educated man, and I still don't know what "capital gains" means.

Adam Gopnik: The Man Who Knows Everything.

(Later, caught the repetition, but let it ride.)

18

I've had it with fiction, whether it's movies, novels, short stories, dramas, whatever.

19

It's a terrible thing to feel you're wasting your time.

20

I wonder how many remember what it was like not to have a remote.

21

I like a coke that has sat,

And has become unbubbly and flat.

I am beginning to have a dislike for Joyce Carol Oates.

I have no earthly or legitimate reason to do so, as I've never read a word of her work nor a sentence of her critiques.

Maybe it's just because she seems to be all over the place, and somehow always in your face.

23

We are to the future what old film clips of people milling about the streets of New York in 1904 are to us.

#22

Another One

Zadie Smith

#18

Of course there is **good** fiction.

I wonder if any is being written these days.

26

The virtue of being unaspectual is that I can now draw upon and meld any aspect of my work.

27

From non-existence I came,

To non-existence I go.

My good friend Nancy told me the other day: "The work of the elderly is to keep going until the next sunrise; that is their **JOB**."

29

By rights, I should have been dead quite a few times ago.

A thin-crusted pizza with the following: pepperoni, mushrooms, green peppers, and pineapple.

The perfect balance.

Orthopedists, cardiologists, ophthalmologists, dermatologists, podiatrists… **Yes!**

Urologists: a pretty sorry crew.

32

Flowers

Their sex lives are very interesting.

But I love flowers because they're beautiful.

I wish I knew how to promote myself.

(Sort of like what Walt Whitman did.)

(Or Robert De Niro in "The King of Comedy.")

34

Senator Mitch McConnell: The Undertaker.

What makes life worth living is essentially this—**surprises**.

I wonder if there are as many sexual scenarios as there are gastronomic ones.

Oh how much we have probably missed out on over the years!

37

The blind, the maimed, the disfigured, amputees, accident victims, invalids, the dismally diseased: I think about them quite often.

38

For a long long time, I thought that big money would unlock just about any door.

I think now just a precious few.

39

I can't get over how **different** siblings can be.

40

What terrible prices are paid for a moment's indiscretion.

41

There should be such a noun as "irrepression."

Once, in Rhodos, there was a Greek-American who had been there for many years. His Greek was so good, you could never tell he wasn't a genuine native.

But one day he gave himself away.

It was an occasion when a friend asked him what flavor of ice cream he wanted.

And he made the fatal mistake of saying, instead of "**sokoláta**," the give-away "**<u>ch</u>okoláta**."

43

I'm tempted to write something putdownish, and even nasty, about Picasso and attendant company, but I guess I'll defer to all the universal, international brouhaha.

The most vulgar, cutthroat, criminal hoodlum who would just as soon slash and shoot a victim at a moment's provocation—many such languishing in maximum security prisons.

Unless you have come to some sort of terms with such an individual, you somehow have not yet arrived.

45

How a Brooklyn bum like Durocher could have stayed married for twelve years to an austere Mormon like Laraine Day is something of a mystery to me.

Someone needs to explain.

Not long ago, it came to my attention that Father Mario Pezzotti of the Missionarios Xaverianos has been classified as a Sexual Predator.

All I can say is that from my experience, Father Mario would not knowingly hurt a flea, much less a small child.

I try to give A's only when they're well-deserved.

48

Reviewers are sometimes such shits.

Pronouncing something bad when it's good, and something good when it's bad.

49

Sometimes I like the Man, but not the Writer.

And vice versa.

49

The same can be said for the Man, and his Voice.

51

All this preoccupation with actors.

When it's probably the writers and directors who deserve the foremost credit.

52

The early early years and these later later years seem to be coalescing.

53

Once, in Frankfurt, I so much regret screaming at the manager of a Volkswagen dealership for not having fixed my car properly and on time.

Since we somehow have gotten onto a confessional mode, one other incident needs recounting.

Once in conversing with a fellow soldier (I think he was), I made the smart-ass and predictable groupie remark that a certain neighborhood of New York was too full of Puerto Ricans. Whereupon my acquaintance replied, "I am a Puerto Rican."

Stammering and apologetic, I suddenly found myself shrinking down to the size of a pea.

Senator Mitch McConnell: The Mortician.

56

What terrible prices are paid for a moment's forgetfulness.

Texas Senatorial Muck

Actually, Cornyn irritates me even more than Ted Cruz.

58

What troubles me is that I have not **earned** the enormous technological strides of mankind.

59

I disliked Trump long before he even thought about running for President.

60

The interesting thing about my writing these days is that it doesn't make the slightest damned difference to me whom I placate and whom I offend.

Whenever I hear a serious reference to **President** Donald Trump, I find myself lapsing into giggles.

62

Equestrian accidents (Cole Porter, Christopher Reeve...) are somewhat foolish, tragic, and uncalled-for.

63

I forgot to add **Brief Encounter** to my list of excellent films.

64

Senator John Cornyn of Texas: a big lumbering Republican oaf.

65

The mark of an inferior man: tattoo.

What appalling violence on this planet, when it so easily could be accord and harmony.

67

Anyone who doesn't see the beauty of dark, rumbling rain-threatening clouds is missing something.

68

I always had a penchant for **exactness**, for honing even minor things to a near-perfection.

I am now losing this obsession, both voluntarily and involuntarily.

69

I have made it abundantly clear, more than once I suspect, that any dramatization of a Jules Verne character or of Nero Wolfe doesn't interest me in the least.

I now also add Inspector Maigret.

When are you going to learn not to touch hot surfaces?

So many bad people: so many Republicans.

Always in a cloud.   Confused and uncertain. From beginning to end.

It's so rare when things are at a certain **equilibrium**: no pain, no anxiety, no worry, no fretfulness, no petulance, no hunger—just muse and wonder.

74

The best wristwatch I've ever had is my current Timex.

52

Stages seem to be supplanting stages in whirlwind fashion.

I never thought I'd find myself ever writing a line like this: The Sports Page of the paper these days is good for wrapping fish.

There are friendships so special and intense that they seem to transcend time and age and even death itself. I'm thinking now of two in particular: how Old Costa and I would go hunting together for vegetarian restaurants around Omonia Square; and Beverly, if she is still with us, who would remember the downpour that afternoon in Torino and the unforgettable night of the assassination in '63.

How delightful and how rare it is to watch a documentary without narration.

79

I remember Ianni Othitis in Hampton, Virginia who would always carry about $4,000 in cash in his bulging wallet.

And Chris Couppis who used to walk 50 blocks or so to his waiter's job in New York to save the subway fare (1950's).

And bulging-eyed Haralambos (or was it his brother Costa?) Kolantis who used to eat a dozen bananas every day for lunch.

And Emily from Aydin who would entertain assembled company by strumming her nose like a guitar.

80

There's something close to immoral about dubbed films.

I Like; I Do Not Like.
Based on having lived a pensive and ruminating lifetime.

My Personal Mantra.

I guess we have to take along our memories when we go.

I don't suppose we could leave them behind.

In 1981 I visited Srinagar and spent a fortnight with the Suri family, Mr. Suri and his wife the botanist "Pinni" Suri, and their delightful daughter Vandana, and her younger brothers Raju and Sanju, and the grandparents Mr. and Mrs. Lall, and Pinni's father Mr. Kohli.

And one day I invited the whole family to dinner on my rented houseboat on Lake Nagin. And I will never forget the elderly Mr. Lall lamenting how filthy Lake Nagin had become and how he remembered swimming there in pristine waters when he was a boy.

And that was nearly 40 years ago.

The most perfect book ever written: **All Trivia** by Logan Pearsall Smith.

85

I didn't know so many sycophants could come creeping out of the woodwork.

Donald Trump

I don't like the way he purses his lips when he
spouts all those banalities.

87

I resent doctors who don't bother to tell you about risks and side effects.

88

There have been times when I have been wrong, self-righteous, and obnoxious.

89

Just think of it: soon there will be no pleasure and pain; no left and right; no up and down; no 1,2,3,4…; no far and near; no before, now, and after; no good and bad; no beautiful and ugly; no same and different; no same and other.

What makes my work special is you can't say what it's about.

91

The very first order of business with the
morning paper is to tackle "The Jumble."

Writers don't have to be polite.

93

You want to hear something crazy: lately I've been praying to my mama, who has long been dead now for 36 years, to look after Nona and my daughter Maya.

I just write; I don't lecture, debate, argue, wish to be interviewed, serve on committees, participate on panels, answer questions, offer opinions.

95

All this talk of calories, all these measurements and quantifications, seem very suspect to me.

I've never been much on kissing. Ever since I was a kid, I found it gooey, gluey, and a bit on the repulsive side.

So many Americans love their dogs; I don't understand it, but I'm forced to admit it.

I've never been terribly fond of generals.

What is needed is a Dictator to get rid of all dictators.

98

Two of my favorites: George Patton and Curtis LeMay.

I've always said that **"arní psitó me patátes"** (roast lamb with potatoes) is the Sovereign of all mealdom.

But I am beginning to think a perfect shish kebab may be a viable Pretender.

102

I wonder if any of the higher animals know when they're being patronized?

My greatest virtue: love of truth.

My greatest vice: cowardice.

All my subsequent **Ex Cathedras** are, in great measure, simply extensions of **Amán Amán!**.

105

Ever since the election, one has the feeling that we've all been somehow mistakenly shunted into some strange alternate universe.

106

Technology is so much more interesting than Art.

How **clean** and undefiled a calendar month looks before it occurs.

And how more or less splotchy it invariably becomes.

108

Neil Tyson would tear it to shreds, but **The Day the Earth Stood Still** was still a good film.

I always wanted to take Nona on a horse-drawn buggy right smack in the middle of the Old City of Bombay, and on a ride along Chowpatty; and also to the Peradeniya Gardens in Sri Lanka.

And Maya to the mineralogical museum in Copiapó, Chile.

And Jim and Nancy to Ambato, Ecuador.

There's something about that song **If Ever I Would Leave You** that is just plain stupid.

111

Maybe it's time I got over this thing with the Southern accent.

Was it a waste of time pursuing all those Latin courses at the University of Virginia?

I think it was.

(But I did make a friend, Bob Strong, and found a favorite professor, Mr. Lehman, along the way.)

113

Acting is really an embarrassing profession.

114

How many in this world echo the labors of Sisyphus.

Those scenes in **America America** in which the family of a rich merchant in Constantinople were trying to marry off Stavros to one of their daughters were **so** well done (especially the father, played by Paul Mann), that although everyone was speaking English, you could swear they were speaking Greek.

116

I just decided: I don't think I like Niall Ferguson.

Timing, just the exactly right timing, having to do with all kinds of activities from cooking to cocktails to social episodes to choosing the precise time of day— how neglected and yet how important and how rewarding.

118

Of all the quite numerous music stations available on my television, I invariably and in the end gravitate to "Easy Listening."

Knowledge for just about everyone is so rough and uneven, full of gaping holes and limitations and omissions, high points and innumerable low points, a few insights encased in a much ampler ignorance, and all subservient to **time**.

I wish people wouldn't pretend that it isn't so.

I sometimes wonder whether, instead of writing about general and abstract matters, I shouldn't be writing about terribly personal things, which would probably be mostly understood by a very few, and even more probably only by me.

I could write a book about all the things that were not fairly depicted in my book.

122

I remember the noises of the subway—distinct, shrieking, screaming, rumbling, echoic noises.

123

In my list of the Underrated (**Ex Cathedra XVI # 151**), I forgot to add Georges Simenon.

The New York Review of Books: It's hard to believe there are people so passionately interested in the details and minutiae of such specialized and niche-like subjects.

Not that I disapprove; in fact, a certain admiration.

If I were to be awarded the Nobel Prize, this is the way I would like to be identified in the roster of winners: "United States (Cyprus, Greece, [Turkey])."

126

Fragments, memory lapses, memory forgettings, faulty sequences, inventions and fabrications...

No one was more right about the self than Hume.

127

No matter how hard scriptwriters try, they hardly ever make conversation sound completely natural, whether on the high end or the low.

128

Who knows, as unlikely as it probably is, maybe Trump will morph into a decent and responsible human being.

It's so easy to spot a nervous and self-conscious participant on television.

130

Trump makes me sick the way the travel host Joseph Rosendo makes me sick.

131

When you're really hurting, nothing matters other than you're really hurting.

132

Critics of the future: it's **you** who will have to connect the dots.

One of the stupidest regrets of my life was to check into a second-rate hotel in Ambato **the very first night** after spending nearly two weeks in that sweat-infested and merciless Ecuadorian jungle.

I still can't believe I did that.

134

Time has a way of making everything that happens very local.

135

One Sunday afternoon at Neptune Beach, a life-guard managed to save me from a possible drowning.

I never got to thank him, or even know who it was.

136

I love stories I hear,

Of the punctiliousness and exactitude,

Of Gustave Flaubert.

I guess physicists know what they're talking about.

138

Putting a period inside the quotation marks of a relatively isolated fragment that happens to come at the end of a sentence is illogical.

But since this is the American way, I guess we just have to follow the rules.

It isn't sensations and sense experience that are explainable by, derivative of, reducible to atoms, electrons, electromagnetic waves, what have you, but the other way around.

When will scientists accept this fundamental truth?

Philosophers have long been mixing ordinary language and figurative (literary) language with reckless abandon, and causing all sorts of confusion.

141

Why has it taken me nearly 87 years to realize certain things?

.

142

All these newscasters, so comfortably ensconced in their hermetic studios, reporting on the horrendous suffering of so many hapless victims.

I never could understand all the **extraordinary** value put on diamonds, rubies, emeralds, gold, etc.

And certainly not as apparel.

Especially if there is pain and evil in their procurement.

Beautiful to look at and think about their rarity, yes. (Almost equally so, their less valuable and identical-looking substitutes.)

I can think of so many other things that merit greater devotion and admiration.

144

I've never detected any genuine and naked malice or prejudice in any member of my family or extended family, or, for that matter, in any Cypriot I have ever personally known.

I remember how mortified I was that day, these ages ago, when I was more or less goaded to boyishly sing **Down Argentina Way**, the lyrics of which I had memorized, in front of assembled family and friends.

"In a minute there is time

For decisions and revisions which a minute will reverse."

Probably the most melodious, intellectually pregnant, and resonating line of all literature.

The Staten Island Ferry

For me, always a treasured memory.

I must admit, I liked tremendously that final barroom gunfighter scene in "Shane."

Shane to Jack Palance: "So you're Jack Wilson."

Jack Palance to Shane: "What's that mean to you Shane?"

Shane to Jack Palance: "I've heard about you."

Jack Palance to Shane: "What have you heard Shane?"

Shane to Jack Palance: "I've heard that you're a low-down Yankee liar."

Jack Palance to Shane: "Prove it."

And then the denouement.

Does it make me glad a hurricane is not coming my way, but going somewhere else?

Answer: yes.

150

I sometimes wonder: Is there anything **not** Googleable?

151

I had no idea, until recently, of the awesome powers of the United States President.

152

How astoundingly different is the world of now from the one I was born into.

153

I still stand by everything I said about Nona, in the Section on "Nona,"

Except for the hearing.

154

Can't forget the Camel smoke rings and Johnnie Walker billboard sign of Times Square.

Or the illuminated Jack Frost beacon in the distance and across the river in the far-off Jersey shore.

The Gardens of Versailles: My soul screams for a wilder and more haphazard landscape.

156

I can just imagine the fun and games analytic philosophers would have with the question of "Who's buried in Grant's Tomb?"

I drive a car, but have very little idea of how it works.

This is true of practically everything I use.

I am not exactly proud of this deficiency.

158

I love the history of technology (and science), but am such a poor devotee to appreciate it.

159

Marooned alone on a tropical desert island without any sort of tool or artifact, I would probably be able to reach low-lying bananas, if any.

And that's about as far as I could get.

#159

Unlike Cyrus Harding in **The Mysterious Island**.

I'm still enamored of the idea that just **thinking the right thought** could get you through to The Aliens.

Now if only one could unearth the right thought.

Leopold II

What sort of human excrement would do the things that he did in the Belgian Congo?

163

There is a crying and desperate need for a
benevolent and competent Planetary Authority that will
supervene all creeds, religions, racial tensions,
timeworn cultural persuasions, national enmities and
aspirations.

Melpo, my favorite aunt: How can I ever forget her kindness, gentleness, and the ever warmth of her receptions.

Peter Joannides

I wouldn't be at all surprised if there isn't a direct lineal genealogical line to Epicurus.

If not to Epicurus, then to Democritus.

166

How sad to say this when I think back on my youthful excitement and glee before taking a trip to new and unchartered destinations:

Every place is more or less like every other place.

One evening, many years ago, while being invited to dinner by a good lady friend of the family, I told our hostess, apropos of nothing in particular, that her **spanakópites** were excellent, some of the best I ever had, but that they were not quite quite as good as those of another lady, also a good friend of the family.

Can you imagine doing anything as imbecilic as this?

It seems that Al Franken is a better senator than he was a comedian.

169

Isn't it a shame that when something gets cracked, it can't be put back together, no matter how closely it approximates, to the way it originally was.

170

I like the science-fiction idea of instant vaporization. No pain or fear. Thugs, dictators, criminals, both blue- and white-collar, just won't know what hit them.

St. Helena: population about 4,000.

Tristan da Cunha: population about 300.

I leave it to you to guess which society tends toward the more moronic.

The template for a bad movie: **Creature from the Black Lagoon**.

173

The other day I watched a large dead oak tree cut down and removed from our yard.

I will never again say anything nasty about a chain saw.

174

Interviewees on so many documentaries seem so very much **alive**; and yet all along I know they've all been long dead.

The poor individual: no choice whatever as to when he was born, to whom he was born, what family, what country, what language, what economic milieu, what era, what genetic traits and dispositions, what grooves are to unfold before him, what accidents and paths await him...

Is there a one who can transcend, just possibly **transcend**, such bone-crushing weights?

176

Good luck is the only thing one can legitimately claim for oneself.

177

I like going in any direction I please.

"To have squeezed the universe into a ball

To roll it toward some overwhelming question,"

What I have been mostly trying to achieve, in these my probably last testaments.

Given the brevities of my format,

Not an easy thing to do.

179

There's something about bees and butterflies slowly savoring and pollinating and flitting from flower to blooming flower that this time gladdens my soul.

My memory is slowly deserting me.

(Even though it seems to have flashes of utter clarity.)

181

How in the world did the American people, all of his millions and billions notwithstanding, manage to elect a President from the gutter?

I really am getting tired and would like to get off the subject of Trump, and politics generally.

I love the air of commentators who seem so cocksure, independent-minded, resolute, and combative...

And the next day might be fired by their superiors.

See **Ex Cathedra XXVI, # 199**.

Time-lapse Photography

Fascinating for flowers, snails, tortoises, strangling vines, disintegrating carcasses, mushrooms and fungi, seasonal forests, construction of a mega-building, traffic patterns, cityscapes, a beautiful and renowned actress as she went from a baby age to a worn and senescent 95…

All this sexual-harassment furor lately is a bit overblown.

It's one thing to attack a woman who obviously becomes a victim. (**Ex Cathedra 11, # 49**: "Nothing more lamebrained than to keep trying to have sex with someone who just isn't interested.")

It's quite another to cajole, entreat, beg, persuade, become a bit forceful.

Half-consensual is very different from non-consensual.

I'm glad I was able to date my students before all this modern self-righteousness set in.

186

The Greek is more and more seeping into my consciousness.

54

Once, with Maya on a ferryboat plying the Greek islands, and full of tourists and natives, Maya suddenly realizes she has mislaid her wallet. Panic and consternation. After a while an announcement on the loudspeaker for someone to come and claim the lost item. Rushing to the reception desk and showing my identification and retrieving the lost wallet, the first thing I blurted out to the purser was "I guess it was a tourist who turned it in." And the reply, "No, it was a Greek."

Once again "…down to the size of a pea."

We need something akin to the Drake Equation for life-sustaining planets, to choose our political leaders.

.

Here I am, dealing with politics again, just as I was trying to get off the subject.

But given the recent events that seem to obtrude and press upon my consciousness, I have this to say:

I would encourage Senator(?) Al Franken to consider running for President.

So many topics I write about, people will, except for a few die-hard historians, soon forget.

(Sort of like H.L. Mencken's **Prejudices, First Series**.)

All religions are ridiculous, except the Greek Orthodox.

And that too is ridiculous in English.

What enormous and hidden twists and complications are sustained by some dual-languaged individuals.

Ex Cathedra XXVI # 80

I've been thinking about what I said not long ago.

I am now beginning to think that there are probably as many musical (sound) possibilities as there are words and sentences and paragraphs and meanings.

Napoleon admired Goethe.

Am I supposed to do cartwheels now?

Nietzsche admired Goethe.

I think I will do cartwheels now.

One time, long ago, Ben Guzzone and I decided we would play two 21-point games, one handball and one racquetball. The winner would be the one with the most points.

We played handball and Ben got 3 points.

We played racquetball and I got 0 points.

One time, long ago, I played two games with a fellow named Gerry Greenside. Neither one of us was in the league of a Jimmy Jacobs or a Naty Alvarado, but on our own level of competence we were not all that far apart. Gerry gave me the worst drubbing I can remember. As the old expression goes, he "beat me like a drum." I think I scored something like 2 and 6. I don't think I was so bad and I don't think he was so much better, but somehow he latched on to my weaknesses and played me as smartly as he could. The score should have been more respectable, even if I were to lose.

It was the most humiliating defeat of all my handball days.

196

The lack of brisk walking, and little socializing, and no travel, and absent and long-gone friends, and physical infirmities and limitations—are beginning to wear on me.

Why do some science writers with their voluminous books full of probably correct facts and arguments and enthusiastically imagined possibilities also seem so unreadable and idiotic?

Back to Kierkegaard again and the two varieties of derangement.

(The play may be quite accurate, but the whole performance may be wrong.)

198

The Times Atlas of the World, by John Bartholomew. Let's face it. It has been my doing and my undoing.

I wonder if **entity** is the most abstract idea that can be.

200

Sometimes I dare myself to say, "I've said enough and have nothing more to say."